BURGHLEY

Stamford Lincolnshire PE9 3JY

Telephone 01780 752451

Fax 01780 480125

email: burghley@burghley.co.uk

www.burghley.co.uk

Opposite:
Verrio's painted ceiling in the Third George Room.

BURGHLEY

STAMFORD • LINCOLNSHIRE

Orlando and Miranda Rock and family

Welcome to Burghley. This palatial Elizabethan prodigy house, with its dramatic skyline and towering obelisk clock tower, was built by my ancestor William Cecil, 1st Lord Burghley and Treasurer to Queen Elizabeth I. Imposing, not to say intimidating from afar, Burghley was built to impress – and the State Rooms on the first floor are awe-inspiring, as they were intended to be. But Burghley is also still a much loved family home and we are incredibly privileged to live here with our children in the ground floor apartments surrounded by Capability Brown's landscape.

Burghley is perhaps best-known for its historic collections of paintings, ceramics and works of art, many of which still stand where they were first recorded in 1688. The extensive archival records – which keep on yielding new discoveries - are key to our understanding of the tastes, traditions and aspirations of past generations.

The House is supported by a vibrant community and working estate involving expertise in many areas including forestry and farming, curatorship, conservation, maintenance of historic buildings and education. It is thanks to this dedication and love for this magical place that it looks as good as it does today.

Thank you for coming to see us. I hope that you have a wonderful day and that you will keep coming back to see Burghley evolve in the years to come. It is with your continued support that the Burghley House Preservation Trust can continue its work to preserve Lord Burghley's ambitious vision for the future.

Miranda Rock

BURGHLEY

CONTENTS

Lancelot 'Capability' Brown – who made his mark on many aspects of Burghley's design, decoration and structure – is seen in this affectionate portrait by Sir Nathaniel Dance at the entrance to one of the Pagoda room's two charming closets.

This single sheet of vellum bearing the Great Seal of England, is the Royal Grant by which Sir William Cecil was created Lord Burghley by Queen Elizabeth I. It is embellished with a coloured miniature, designed by Nicholas Hilliard (1547–1619), of the enthroned Queen holding the sceptre and orb.

THE BUILDER OF THE HOUSE

WILLIAM CECIL LORD BURGHLEY

1520–1598

He was involved in the downfall of the Lord Protector Somerset and was in some personal danger during the repressive reign of Mary I but contrived to give support and encouragement to Princess Elizabeth. At her succession in 1558, she repaid his loyalty by making him her principal Secretary and later Lord Treasurer.

Elizabeth I, by Marcus Gheeraerts the Younger (1561–1636) (Pagoda Room).

William Cecil founded a dynasty at Burghley from which place he took his title and built himself a palace commensurate with his importance. His elder son was created Earl of Exeter and his descendants have lived here ever since.

At his death he was described by Lord Essex in a letter to Queen Elizabeth as *'The greatest, gravest and most esteemed Councillor that ever Your Majesty had'*.

Burghley's effigy in St Martin's Church, Stamford shows him in full armour, and if this seems incongruous in a Lord Treasurer and Chief Minister, the great historian of the Elizabethan age, E. M. Tenison, comments: *'That he was our greatest War Minister is a revelation even to his own descendants . . . he had not only studied war from the Marshal's Court but also in the fighting line'*.

William Cecil, Lord Burghley in the robes of a Knight of The Garter, holding his wand of office, by Marcus Gheeraerts the Younger (1561–1636) (Pagoda Room).

A view of Burghley from the West drawn by John Haynes, 1755.

Detail of a view of Burghley, by Caldwell c. 1720, from the South showing the Garden prior to 'Capability' Brown's alterations.

THE HISTORY OF BURGHLEY

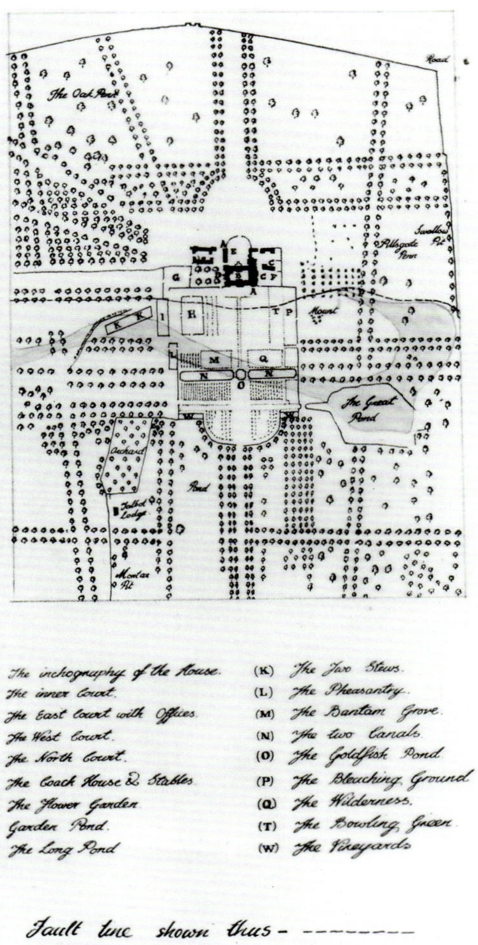

An architect's re-drawing of John Haynes's plan of 1755.

The building period of the House extended over 32 years. We know from the State Papers that the East range was erected in 1555.

Work on the East and South ranges continued until 1564. Sir William Cecil (as he was, until ennobled in 1571), had purchased Theobalds Manor, Hertfordshire in 1563 and for a whole decade was fully engaged there in the building of his great 'prodigy' house. At Burghley in August 1564, Edmund Hall, the surveyor, promised that the South side should be finished by winter. Thereafter, little more work was done until 1575 when the team of masons was reassembled (their combined wages were £11.00 weekly). The West front with its great gate-house (it was originally intended to be the main entrance) was finished in 1577. The North front was completed in 1587.

A view of the Inner Court at Burghley by John Haynes, 1755.

There can be little doubt that William Cecil was his own architect, apart from help in design and execution by an Antwerp mason named Henryk (certain columns and decorated fittings for a gallery were prefabricated and sent over ready for assembly). Cecil collected through agents abroad all available new works on architecture. His correspondence shows that he could and did supply a 'tryke' (drawing) of some detail at the request of his master mason. The stone used was from the local quarry of Northamptonshire oolitic limestone at Kingscliffe - so hard and of such durability that even on the South front, fully a quarter of the ashlar (sawn) blocks still show masons' identifying marks. There is evidence to suggest that the Great Hall was rebuilt on a grander scale during the initial building period. Also the West front gate-house with its four turrets and additional storey, dwarfed the East front inner courtyard porch, which was given an extra clock stage and crowned with a massive 'obelisk', accounting for the late date thereon of 1585 (left).

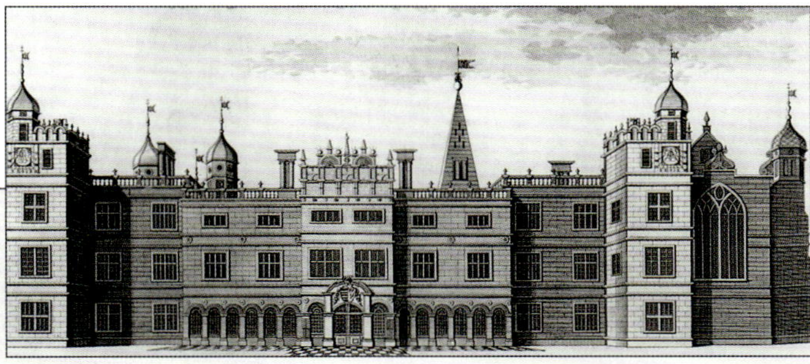

An engraving, by an unknown artist, showing the South front of Burghley, c. 1750, prior to Brown's alterations.

Lancelot 'Capability' Brown's drawing of the South front of Burghley House c. 1760, showing two options for alterations to the roof line.

At some time in the late 17th century, the open gallery on the South front was enclosed and altered considerably. It is tempting to think that this was as a result of damage caused by Cromwell's bombardment before he stormed the house in July 1643. In 1683, the 5th Earl inserted large mullioned windows on the South and West fronts and a segmental pedimented entrance on the South front. Under the supervision of the 9th Earl, 'Capability' Brown, from 1756 to 1779 made considerable architectural alterations and additions, raising the roof line of the South front to give an even skyline. In addition, he built the stable courtyard and the Orangery in the 1760s and the Lion Bridge over the lake in 1775. At Brown's suggestion, the North West low wing was removed in the 1760s to open up the view. Brown also landscaped the gardens and park and advised the Earl on interior decorations. In 1828, the 2nd Marquess employed J.P. Gandy to construct a two-storey corridor round the inner courtyard (single storey at the East side).

The South front of Burghley House.

THE CECILS OF BURGHLEY

The Cecils originated in Herefordshire. A younger son, David, settled in Stamford and married the daughter of a local minor landowner who was thrice Mayor of Stamford.

Dying in 1541, he was succeeded by his son Richard. Both were able lawyers and found employment at Court under Henry VIII and Edward VI. Richard Cecil died in 1552, possessed of estates at Burghley and Wothorpe. Richard's eldest son, **William** (1520–1598), was involved in the downfall of the Lord Protector Somerset and was in some personal danger during the repressive reign of Mary I but contrived to give support and encouragement to Princess Elizabeth. At her succession in 1558, he became Principal Secretary and later Lord Treasurer. He was created Lord Burghley in 1571 and grants of land and Crown offices continued throughout his long life. Burghley's elder son, **Thomas**, became Earl of Exeter in 1605 and the 10th Earl, Henry, became the 1st Marquess in 1801. None of the successors of the 1st Lord Burghley in the senior line became eminent politicians, but two, the 5th and 9th Earls, made considerable alterations to the fabric and contents of the house.

Thomas, 1st Earl of Exeter, *English School c.1610 (Pagoda Room).*

Letters patent creating Thomas, Lord Burghley, Earl of Exeter, with the Royal Arms of King James I.

John, 5th Earl of Exeter *by Sir Godfrey Kneller (1646–1723) (Billiard Room).*

Anne, wife of the 5th Earl *by Sir Godfrey Kneller (1646–1723) (Billiard Room).*

John, 5th Earl, (1648–1700) made at least four long journeys through France and Italy. During these tours he commissioned tapestries, statuary and furniture and purchased a large number of Italian paintings. At home, his patronage included Jean Tijou, the iron worker (West front - Golden Gates) and his son-in-law, Louis Laguerre, the decorative painter (the Bow Room); Antonio Verrio, who worked from 1686–1697 on the George Rooms; Grinling Gibbons and the school of wood carvers who emulated his work; John Vanderbank who was weaving tapestries for him some years before he was established in London; Edward Martens, who modelled over twenty lovely baroque ceilings and many other English painters, poets and craftsmen.

John, 6th Earl of Exeter.
(1674–1721) Little is known about this Earl although it might be suspected that he spent his whole life worrying about the enormous debts left behind by his father. He married twice, the first time for less than a year, his wife died without issue; the second time to Elizabeth Brownlow of nearby Belton House, who bore him five sons and one daughter.

John, 7th Earl of Exeter.
(1700–1722) Son of the Sixth Earl, the Seventh Earl died unmarried, a few months after succeeding to the title.

Brownlow, 8th Earl of Exeter.
(1701–1754) Brother of the Seventh Earl, Brownlow married an heiress, Hannah-Sophia Chambers, to whom we are indebted for the existence of the enormous silver wine cooler in the Great Hall. It had been ordered by the Fifth Earl but it could not be paid for until Hannah-Sophia's father, delighted with his daughter's marriage into the aristocracy, settled the account.

Henry, 10th Earl and 1st Marquess of Exeter
with his wife, Sarah and their daughter Lady Sophia Cecil by Sir Thomas Lawrence (1769–1830) (Billard room).

His great-grandson, **Brownlow, 9th Earl** (1725–1793), completed the renovation and furnishings of the first floor State Rooms (known as the George Rooms from the 17th century). They had remained in an unfinished state for over fifty years. Although the Earl was a modern man and adopted the Neo-classical style of decoration which appeared in England in the 1760s, he firmly retained the decorative painting, baroque ceilings and carved cornices, jambs and overdoors from the 5th Earl's time and married them to carved detail derived from the great folios of measured drawings of classical ruins which were published from 1753 onwards.

Brownlow, 9th Earl of Exeter
by Angelica Kauffmann (1741–1807) (Pagoda Room)

The Burghley Bowl. This 18th century Chinese export bowl (c. 1738) shows the south front as it was in 1754 when the 9th Earl inherited the title, and prior to the refenestration and levelling of the skyline carried out by Capability Brown.

He too, spent long periods in Italy, collecting large numbers of works of art. The 9th Earl was succeeded by his nephew, **Henry, 10th Earl** (1754–1804), who was elevated to the rank of Marquess in 1801. To celebrate, he built the magnificent Bottle Lodges. He separated from his first wife and subsequently met and married in unusual and romantic circumstances a beautiful peasant girl called Sarah Hoggins. This unlikely romance was celebrated by the poet Tennyson, in his ballad *The Lord of Burghley*. Sarah, known as 'The Cottage Countess', bore her husband three children but their happy marriage was cut short by her death in 1797. Sarah never lived to become a Marchioness but Lord Exeter married a third time, to the dowager Duchess of Hamilton.

The **2nd Marquess** (1795–1867) entertained on a lavish scale at Burghley - the Duchess of Kent and her daughter, Princess Victoria in 1835, the Queen Dowager (Adelaide, widow of William IV) in 1842 and again Victoria in 1844 but this time as Queen. Throughout this period came a heavy outlay on furnishings and fittings.

The **3rd Marquess of Exeter** (1825–1895) was a Member of Parliament for South Lincolnshire from 1847 to 1857 and became a Privy Councillor and ADC to Queen Victoria. He married Lady Georgina Pakenham, a daughter of the 2nd Earl of Longford.

Like his father, the **4th Marquess** (1849–1898) was a Member of Parliament and a Privy Councillor before succeeding to the peerage. He was Vice-Chamberlain to Queen Victoria in 1891. He married Isabella, only child and heiress of Sir Thomas Whichcote, 7th Baronet of Aswarby Park, Lincolnshire.

The **5th Marquess** (1876–1956) succeeded in 1898 and died in 1956, an interval embracing both World Wars, each followed by prolonged agricultural depression. He carefully nursed the estate through these difficult times and achieved a great reputation in public service. Lord Exeter was a Knight of the Garter and Hereditary Grand Almoner, and Lord Lieutenant of Northamptonshire from 1922 to 1951. For 11 years he was ADC to King George V and played a large part in local affairs, being Mayor of Stamford in 1909 and spokesman for the community as well as being chairman of local charities, a J.P. and *Custos Rotulorum* for the Soke of Peterborough. He married the Hon. Myra Orde-Powlett, only daughter of the 4th Lord Bolton. He was succeeded by his elder son.

The **6th Marquess** (1905–1981) achieved, as Lord Burghley, an international reputation as a hurdler between 1924 and 1933, winning a gold medal in the Olympic 400 metres hurdles at Amsterdam in 1928 and a silver medal in Los Angeles in 1932. His enthusiasm for promoting amateur sport after the war was expressed in his work as President of the Amateur Athletics Association, President of the International Amateur Athletics Federation and membership of the International Olympic Committee. He staged the 1948 Olympic Games in London with great success under difficult conditions. From 1943 to 1945 he was Governor and C.-in-C. Bermuda and established the Burghley Horse Trials in 1961.

The **7th Marquess of Exeter** (1909–1988) was educated at Dartmouth R.N. College, subsequently serving in the Royal Navy. He left England for Canada as a young man, to run the ranch purchased by his father before the Great War.

The 7th Marquess was succeeded by his only son **Michael, 8th and present Marquess**. Lord Exeter is father to Anthony, Lord Burghley and Lady Angela Cecil, who sadly died in 2008. Lord and Lady Exeter currently live in the United States but still find time to visit Burghley and keep in touch with events in England.

The CECILS *of* Burghley

Mary Cheke (1) — **William Cecil, Lord Burghley, KG*** (1520–1598) — (2) Mildred Cooke

Thomas, 1st Earl of Exeter, KG* (1542–1622) — Dorothy Nevill

Robert Cecil
1st Earl of Salisbury

The Marquesses of Salisbury, of Hatfield House

William, 2nd Earl of Exeter (1566–1640) (d.s.p.m.s)

Sir Richard Cecil (1570–1633) — Elizabeth Cope

David, 3rd Earl of Exeter (d.1643) — Lady Elizabeth Egerton

John, 4th Earl of Exeter (1628–1678) — Lady Frances Manners

John, 5th Earl of Exeter* (1648–1700) — Lady Anne Cavendish*

(d.s.p.)	died sine prole (without issue)
(d.s.p.m.s)	died without surving male issue
KG	Knight of the Garter
KCMG	Knight Commander of the Order of St.Michael and St. George
KCVO	Knight Commander of the Royal Victorian Order
CVO	Commander of the Royal Victorian Order
DL	Deputy Lieutenant
*	illustrated here

John, 6th Earl of Exeter (1674–1721) — Elizabeth Brownlow

John, 7th Earl of Exeter (1700–1722)

Brownlow, 8th Earl of Exeter (1701–1754) — Hannah-Sophia Chambers

Laetitia Townsend* (1) — **Brownlow, 9th Earl of Exeter*** (1725–1793) (d.s.p.) — (2) Anne Cheatham

Thomas Chambers Cecil (1728–1778) — Charlotte Gornier

Emma Vernon (1) — **Henry, 10th Earl and 1st Marquess of Exeter*** (1754–1804) — (2) Sarah Hoggins* (The Cottage Countess)

Brownlow, 2nd Marquess of Exeter, KG (1795–1867) — Isabella Poyntz*

William Alleyne, 3rd Marquess of Exeter (1825–1895) — Lady Georgina Pakenham

Brownlow, 4th Marquess of Exeter (1849–1898) — Isabella Whichcote

William, 5th Marquess of Exeter, KG (1876–1956) — Hon. Myra Orde-Powlett*

Lady Mary Montagu Douglas Scott (1) — **David, 6th Marquess of Exeter KCMG*** (1905–1981) — (2) Diana Henderson

Edith Csanady de Telegd (1) — **Martin, 7th Marquess of Exeter** (1909–1988) — (2) Lillian Johnson

John (d. an infant)

Lady Davina — 11th Lord Barnard

Sir Giles Floyd Bt.(1) — Lady Gillian — (2) George Kertesz (3) Jeremy Smith

Sir Michael Oswald, KCVO — Lady Angela CVO

Lady Victoria DL — Simon Leatham

Nancy Meeker (1) — **Michael, 8th Marquess of Exeter** — (2)Barbara Coffman

Lady Marina — Peter Castonguey

Harry, Carolyn, Elizabeth, Sophia, Louise

David, Henry

William, Katharine

Richard, Miranda

Anthony Lord Burghley (b.1970) — Holly Stewart

Lady Angela

Dylan (d.s.p.), Majessa

The Grand Tourists

During the late 17th century the reign of John, the 5th Earl and his Countess, Anne transformed and embellished Burghley House beyond recognition.

Lord Exeter's considerable taste was greatly aided by marrying a considerable heiress, Anne Cavendish, daughter of the 3rd Earl of Devonshire. The couple shared a passion for beautiful things and a lust for travel. They were among the first 'Grand Tourists' and travelled to the great cultural centres of Europe on four separate occasions, collecting important paintings (over 300), tapestries, sculptures and objects of virtue. These found their way back to Burghley House along with artists and decorators from the Continent such as the Parisian, Jean Tijou, who created the Golden Gates we see today, and painters such as the Italian, Verrio, who was responsible for most of the magnificent painted ceilings in the house. The refurbishment and alteration of Burghley was carried out almost on a royal scale and the expenditure was enormous. Both the Earl and Countess died with over £8,000 of unsettled debts and this impoverished the estate for the next thirty years. Fortunately the large part of their collections survive at Burghley and can be seen by visitors as a unique example of the tastes of a 17th century nobleman and his Countess.

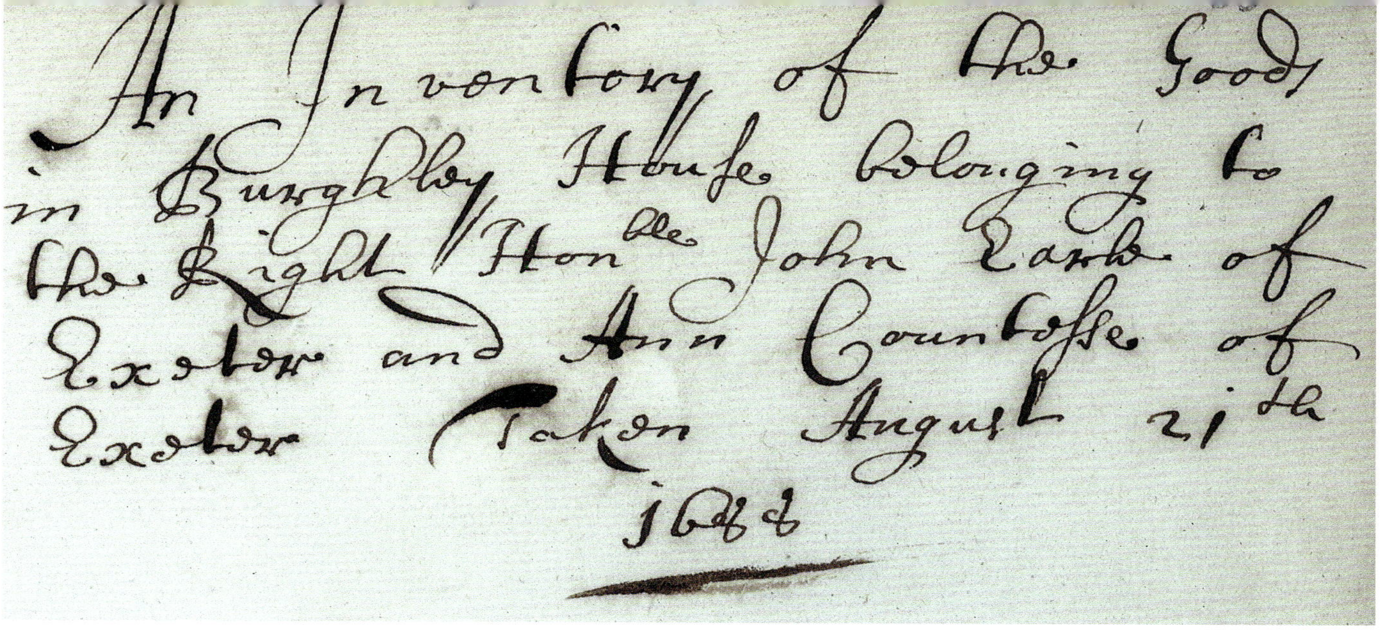

The extended foreign journeys of John and his Countess, together with the presence of so many craftsmen and builders in the house were probably amongst the reasons behind the preparation of a detailed inventory of the contents in 1688.

*A detail of the title page from the first inventory to be drawn up at Burghley, '**An inventory of the goods in Burghley House belonging to the Right Honourable John Earl of Exeter and Ann Countess of Exeter Taken August 21st 1688**'.*

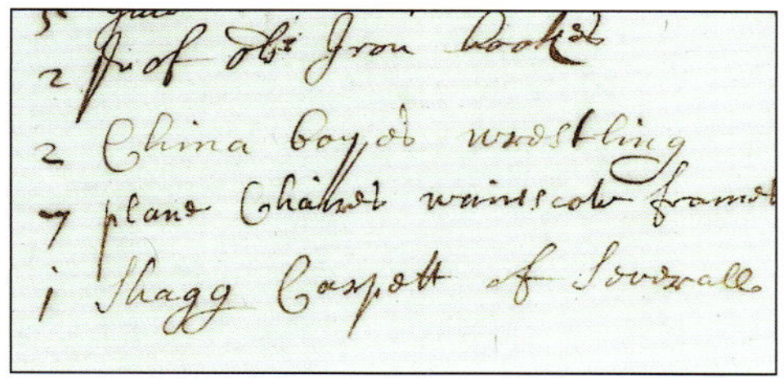

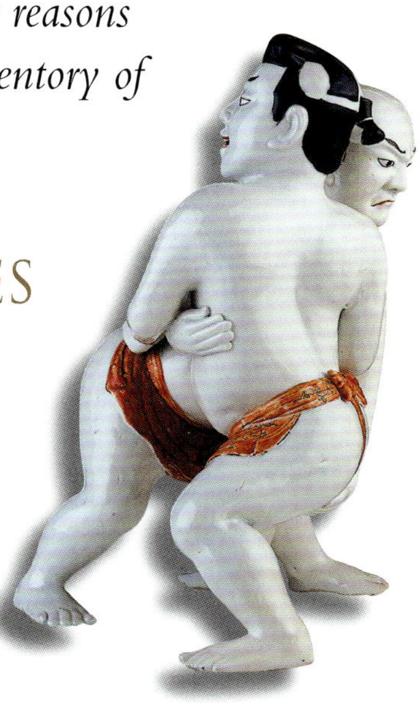

*A page from the first inventory made for the 5th Earl in 1688 by Culpepper Tanner, steward of the household. It itemises furniture, paintings and porcelain. This page (third line), mentions the '**2 china boyes wrestling**' (left), which are still in the collection at Burghley.*

THE EARLY INVENTORIES

This clearly-written document lists furniture, paintings and ceramics. Recent detailed research into the inventory has revealed that many of the objects that are recorded remain in the Collection today. The listing of the Japanese porcelains is the earliest known record of such a collection in the Western world. The 5th Countess's mother, Elizabeth, Countess of Devonshire, died in 1689 and left her daughter an immense inheritance. The entire contents of Elizabeth's apartments at Chatsworth were left to Anne, with the wise proviso that they were "for her peculiar use and benefit. with which the Earl of Exeter should not intermeddle". This was of course many years before the Married Woman's Property Act! The bequest was meticulously listed in a vellum Deed of 1690, known as 'The Devonshire Schedule'. Again, many of the treasures listed remain at Burghley today.

The Devonshire Schedule lists the huge number of precious 'objets de vertu', paintings, miniatures and silver left to Anne Cecil by her mother.

Left: A Spanish gold and enamel horse pendant, circa 1600. Listed in the Devonshire Schedule as: 'Jewels....A Cupid on horseback in Gold enamell'd with a Gold chaine sett with rubies & diamonds and three pendant pearls.' (The figure of Cupid has been missing since the 19th century).

Burghley at a Glance

BURGHLEY

1. Visitor entrance and Brewhouse Centre
2. Car and Coach Park
3. Entrance to State Rooms
4. Orangery Restaurant
5. Gift Shop
6. Garden Shop
7. Garden Café
8. Entrance to the Sculpture Garden and the Garden of Surprises

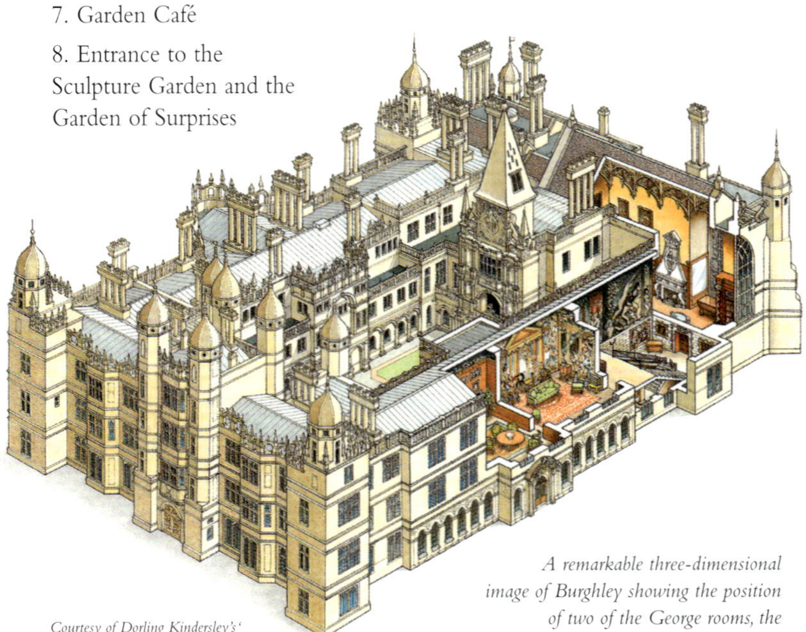

Courtesy of Dorling Kindersley's 'Travel Guide Great Britain'

A remarkable three-dimensional image of Burghley showing the position of two of the George rooms, the Hell Staircase and the Great Hall.

The main part of the house has 35 major rooms on the ground and first floors. There are more than 80 lesser rooms and numerous halls, corridors, bathrooms and service areas. The lead roof extends to three-quarters of an acre. Work on the restoration and rebuilding of the roof began in 1983; the main roof is now completed. Work continues to the surrounding buildings and estate to provide more facilities and enjoyment for visitors.

Burghley is a living house, much work is being done to clean, restore and revive both the structure and the contents. Because of this, the position of items within the house may change. Objects are often loaned to exhibitions both in this country and abroad.

The glass, steel and oak structure of the new entrance pavilion sits comfortably next to the 18th-century Brewhouse.

THE BREWHOUSE VISITOR AND EDUCATION CENTRE

The Brewhouse visitor and education centre opened in May 2006. The original building was designed by Lancelot 'Capability' Brown and formed the slaughterhouse, bake house and brewhouse for the Estate. It lay empty and derelict from the early 20th century, before being restored with the help of the Heritage Lottery Fund. It now provides dedicated spaces for learning and interpretation. The 'Ancestors in the Attic' audio visual display provides a novel and fascinating insight into the history of Burghley and the effect its residents have had on the house over the centuries. An important aspect of the newly refurbished Brewhouse is "The Treasury" gallery on the first floor. This purpose-built display area has given the opportunity for a series of special exhibitions that focus upon areas of the Collection that cannot usually be displayed in the staterooms. In recent years there have been exhibitions of the world famous Burghley collection of Chinese Snuff Bottles, rare Japanese Kakiemon ceramics and a stunning group of treasures from the Elizabethan period.

The Brewhouse Treasury hosts an annual display of items which are not normally on view to visitors.

A TOUR *of the* House

The 'Roman Stairs' lead the Visitor from the ground floor to the tour of the first floor rooms.

ROOMS ON THE TOUR

The tour of the House extends for over 250 metres throughout the ground and first floors, and passes through eighteen rooms, upon the walls of which are nearly 400 paintings.

FIRST FLOOR

GROUND FLOOR

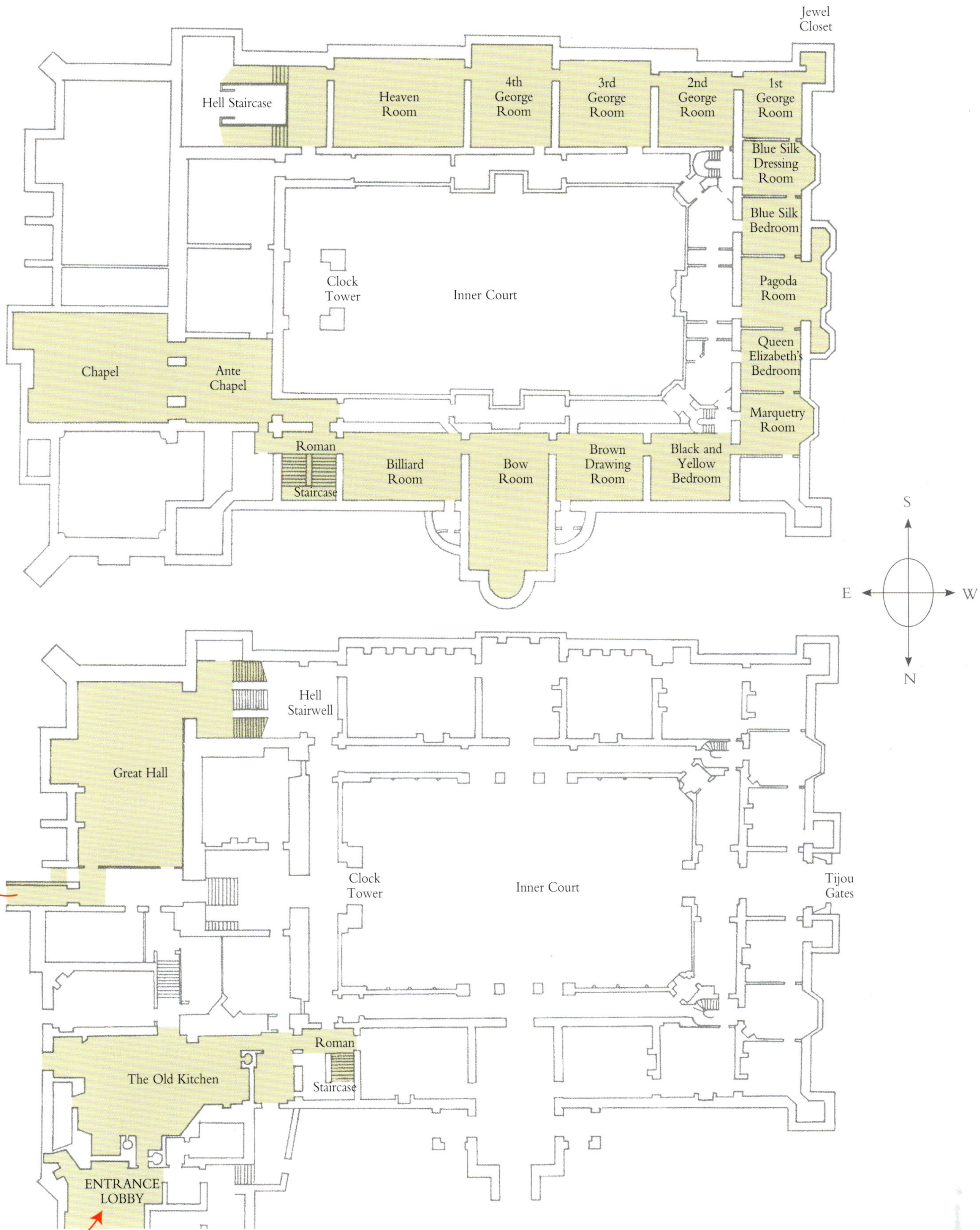

The kitchen is one of the few remaining rooms at Burghley which remind us that the house was built during the Tudor period.

The rib-vaulted roof leads up to a lantern which would have served to extract smoke and fumes from the original fire. The lantern was exposed and restored in 1985, having been concealed within the bathroom of a second floor guest bedroom for many years! The enormous painting of a butchered ox is by Frans Snyders (1579–1657).

The skulls on the wall are those of turtles, brought to the house for the making of turtle soup. They were presumably placed there by a chef who wished to reinforce the message given in the notice that hangs beneath them.

The rib-vaulted roof, and the aperture to release fumes and smoke.

Presumably, the impressive copper turtle tureen was the centrepiece of the table when turtle soup was on the menu.

The fine collection of some 260 copper utensils, from the late Georgian and early Victorian period, gives an idea of the huge meals and extensive entertaining which occurred in country houses at that time. As dentistry was in its infancy, many people suffered from very poor teeth - hence the great range and number of jelly moulds to be seen.

The Hog's Hall houses leather fire buckets, numerous bells and the leather and mahogany Porter's chair.

The Roman Staircase, taken from a view in Nash's 'Mansions of England'.

Leaving the kitchen, visitors pass through the Hog's Hall where there is a collection of early leather fire buckets and numerous bells that would have summoned servants to the furthest reaches of the house. Until the late 1950s the only telephone in the house was situated here - in arctic conditions! Burghley was only connected to mains electricity in 1956; before this all heating and even the lighting was gas fired. The fine staircase, with a coffered ceiling bearing Tudor emblems is known as the Roman Stairs as it is modelled on the Scala Romana of classical architecture; it leads to the Ante-Chapel.

The Ante Chapel

Whilst the family and their guests attended prayers in the Chapel itself, the household staff assembled in this outer room.

On the South wall is a large and rare painting by Antonio Palma (1511-1575) entitled "Coriolanus and the Roman Matrons", purchased by the 5th Earl of Exeter during one of his visits to Italy on the 'Grand Tour', (see page 16 - 'The Grand Tourists') in the late 17th century. To the left is a **square piano** (right) made by Longman and Broderip *circa* 1790 and purchased by the 9th Earl, a keen musician. This delightful instrument was fully restored to playing condition in 1995.

Coriolanus and the Roman matrons by Antonio Palma.

Under the painting by Palma (above), is a French harmonium made by Alexandre et Fils in 1840, upon which is a **large 19th century family bible**.

The plasterwork ceilings of the Ante Chapel and the Chapel were designed for the 9th Earl by Lancelot 'Capability' Brown in the late 18th century. The window on the West side of the room gives the only view from the state rooms of the **Inner Court**.

THE CHAPEL

The room is dominated by the magnificent altarpiece of 'Zebedee's wife petitioning Our Lord' by Paolo Veronese (1529–1583).

Records show that the painting was purchased by the 9th Earl from the Church of San Giacomo on the Venetian island of Murano. The Chapel contains some important furniture. The two mahogany pulpits follow a design by Thomas Chippendale and were made by the London firm of Mayhew and Ince, who also made the splendid mahogany Gothic pews at the front of the Chapel. The more robust pews toward the rear of the room are made from pine and beech wood painted to resemble mahogany, and were possibly designed for the open passages around the ground floor of the house before they were enclosed in 1828. Around the room are ranged ten figures depicting the Wise Virgins. These are made of bronzed plaster, probably by Hardenberg of London and were purchased by the 1st Marquess in 1801. The large scagliola and marble fireplace was removed from a convent near Lisbon by Lord Howard de Walden in the early 19th century and was purchased from him by the 2nd Marquess. Against the fireplace wall is a rare small chamber organ built for the 9th Earl in 1790 by William Gray. Unusually, its case resembles that of a harpsichord.

The 17th century carved swags of fruit and flowers that decorate the walls are in the style of Grinling Gibbons but are probably the work of two of his followers, Jonathan Maine and Thomas Young.

Zebedee's wife petitioning Our Lord by Paolo Veronese.

The Billiard Room

The Billiard Room is characterised by ornate rich Norwegian oak panelling, which gives a dramatic backdrop to the many family portraits inset.

One of the finest pictures is of the 10th Earl and his family by Sir Thomas Lawrence, whose small self-portrait (right), in pencil, is situated near the fireplace. The billiard table was made in the 1850s, the frame being of oak taken from the wreck of the battleship Royal George which sank at Spithead in 1782 and was raised in 1841. On the table are two 'mace' cues, fore-runners of the modern cue. They date from the late 18th century.

Portrait of Henry, 10th Earl and 1st Marquess of Exeter with his wife, Sarah and their daughter Lady Sophia Cecil by Sir Thomas Lawrence (1769–1830).

The row of paintings in oval frames depicts members of the gentlemen's drinking club, known as the '*Little Bedlam Club*', which was based at Burghley in the 17th century. Among its members were Sir Godfrey Kneller (1649–1723), seen here in a rare self-portrait (left), and the artist Antonio Verrio (1639–1707) (right), portrayed by Kneller. Verrio was employed by the 5th Earl to paint a number of rooms at Burghley. The house contains many of his masterpieces including the Heaven Room, the ceilings of the four George Rooms and the Hell Staircase.

A large blue and white jar, Chinese, Ming dynasty, circa 1690. This jar is described in the 1690 Devonshire Schedule.

Lancelot 'Capability' Brown designed the ceiling of this room. His inspiration came from the newly discovered ruins at Palmyra.

The entrance to the Billiard Room from the Roman Stairs. On the left wall in the Billiard Room are six oval portraits depicting members of Burghley's 18th century drinking club, 'The Little Bedlam Club'.

On the east wall is this delightful study in oak of a brace of Woodcock, by a local carver.

THE BOW ROOM

This lofty and imposing room was decorated for the 5th Earl by Louis Laguerre in 1697.

Laguerre, a godson of Louis XIV, depicted episodes from the life of Cleopatra and Mark Antony upon the East and West walls, the Conduct of Scipio towards his Fair Captive on the South wall and scenes from classical mythology on the ceiling. The room was planned as the State Dining Room and is so described in the Inventory of 1688. The 5th Earl must have seen glorious decorated rooms of this kind during his travels in the warm, sunny climes of northern Italy but the creation of such a room, on the North side of the house in chilly Lincolnshire must have meant that grand dinner parties were extremely cold affairs! The 9th Earl used it as a music room and held performances here and in the early part of this century it was used as a secondary billiard room. During 1990 the entire painted decoration was cleaned and restored to great effect, taking 3,000 hours of painstaking work. The dining table is laid as it might have been for a Victorian dinner party. Given the distance from the kitchen, most dishes must have been cool if not cold, making the silver plate warmers essential! The circular drum table at the rear of the room is that at which Benjamin Disraeli, when Prime Minister, drew up the final details of the Congress of Berlin with members of his cabinet in 1878. The blanc de chine porcelain figures on the mantelpiece are 17th century and were listed as being in this position in the 1688 Inventory.

Portraits of Sir Christopher Whichcote, Bt. and Lady Whichcote of Aswarby Park, Lincolnshire by Thomas Gainsborough. They were ancestors of Isabella Whichcote, wife of the 4th Marquess of Exeter.

Rose and Glass by Hermann van der Mijn.

Spaniel and Dead Game by Hermann van der Mijn. It is recorded that this picture was painted in 1730 and that the spaniel was 'Ld Exeter's favourite dog, Diddle'.

THE BROWN DRAWING ROOM

The splendid plaster-work ceiling in this room is one of over twenty in the house that were executed for the 5th Earl by Edward Martens in the late 17th century.

Upon the walls hang many important paintings; particularly notable are the portraits by Thomas Gainsborough (1727–1788), of Sir Christopher and Lady Whichcote, ancestors of the 4th Marchioness (130 and 131), and two superb paintings by Hermann van der Mijn (1684–1741); *Rose in a Glass* and *Spaniel with Dead Game* (527 and 151). The small bed in the room was last used by Queen Victoria when, as a young girl, she visited the house with her mother, the Duchess of Kent, in 1835. It was a rule of her mother's that the young Princess slept in a room adjacent to her own. The wonderful pair of serpentine-fronted, ormolu-mounted mahogany chests-of-drawers are part of a suite of six and date from the middle of the 18th century. Between them are a remarkable mirror and console table. The mirror and table have traditionally been attributed to Mayhew and Ince. The porcelain in this room is mainly 18th century Chinese export-ware. The striking painting on glass framed in the window is by Margaret Pierson, after Wright of Derby and is signed and dated 1789.

During World War II a bomb fell in the park about 200 yards from the house, blowing in all the windows in several rooms on this north front. It is fortunate, therefore, that the painting on glass by Margaret Pierson, survived the action and can still be seen fastened between two window mullions.

BURGHLEY

THE BLACK AND YELLOW BEDROOM

The finely worked state bed dates from the mid-18th century but is made in the style of the Queen Anne period.

The bed was used by King George VI and HM Queen Elizabeth the Queen Mother, then Duke and Duchess of York, when they stayed at Burghley. The hangings were first restored in 1838 and the headboard of the bed bears that date. A major conservation project has taken place in recent years to once again restore the bed to its original glory. The two Soho 'Grotesque' tapestries date from the 17th century and were made by John Vanderbank at the Great Queen Street Workshops in Soho, London. They have been cleaned and repaired and now show much of their original colour.

The painting over the fireplace of Logic between Vice and Virtue (139) is one of the finest works of Pietro Liberi (1614–1687), one of the many great Italian artists patronised by the 5th Earl. The surrounding lime wood carvings are the work of the Gibbons school of carvers of the late 17th century. Between the windows is an unusually large looking-glass with a verre églomisé surround. In the centre of the room is a mahogany breakfast table in the style of Chippendale.

One of the two 17th century 'Grotesques' tapestries made in Soho by John Vanderbank.

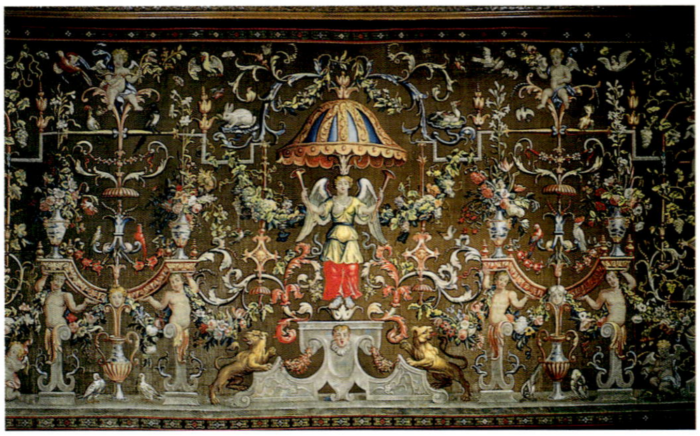

162
476
227
188
3

The Marquetry Room

This room is so called because of the fine examples of marquetry furniture to be seen here.

The large linen press was made up in the early 19th century using 17th century panels of Dutch walnut marquetry. The small chest of drawers also features Dutch marquetry. The painting that dominates this room is the version of Rent Day (609) by Pieter Brueghel the Younger (1564–1638). Alongside it hangs an intricately detailed pearwood carving of a dead bird worked and signed by Jean Demontreuil, a Frenchman renowned for fine carving in the late 18th century. The maiolica plates hanging in the window bay were bought in Italy by the 9th Earl and are examples from the Castelli and Urbino workshops. The series of five rooms along this West side of the house was formed from the original Elizabethan Long Gallery by the 5th Earl during his alterations. They contain many typical 17th century features such as the corner chimneypieces used to display porcelain. These follow a design originated by Daniel Marot (1661–1752). The porcelain display on this chimneypiece is part of the world-famous Burghley collection of Japanese ceramics, much of which is recorded in the 1688 Inventory of the house, thus making it the earliest inventoried collection in the western world. The decoration of this room was renewed in 1989 and incorporates faux marbre (false marble), re-creating the room's design as described in the 1738 Inventory of the house.

Detail from 'Rent Day' by Pieter Brueghel the Younger.

A delicate late 18th century carving of a dead bird by Demontreuil, carved from a single piece of wood, hangs near the door into the next room.

'QUEEN ELIZABETH'S' BEDROOM

Originally part of the Long Gallery, this room has been so called for at least 150 years.

Queen Elizabeth visited William Cecil frequently at his other houses, but when she came to visit Burghley in 1566, she was prevented from staying by an outbreak of smallpox within the household. The superb state bed and the suite of chairs date from the 17th century. They were fully restored in 1985 when the decayed curtain hangings, chair coverings and the bedspread were replaced—all of the textiles were kept as a record—and the rest of the original fabric and trimming cleaned and repaired.

The tapestries, from the Metamorphoses series, were ordered from Jean Jans at the Paris Gobelins factory by the 5th Earl and his Countess whilst touring Europe in 1680. On top of the lacquered chest is an interesting mirror; within the olive-wood veneer surround the English stumpwork features embroidery portrayals of King William and Queen Mary (1688–1702).

The chest and the side table are good examples of 17th century English japanning, an imitation of Oriental lacquer. Following the publication in 1688 of '*A Treatise of Japanning and Varnishing*' by John Stalker & George Parker, japanning became a hobby for ladies of leisure at a time where there was a craze for all things oriental.

One of the Gobelins tapestries, depicting Bacchus & Ariadne. Notice the arms at the top of Cecil impaling Cavendish, representing the 5th Earl and his wife Lady Anne Cavendish, daughter of the 3rd Earl of Devonshire.

Either side of the room are two small closets giving impressions of previous eras in the house.

One of a suite of 18th century English mahogany commodes by John Cobb. Others in the suite may be by Henry Tatham, a Stamford furniture maker who was an apprentice of Cobb.

THE PAGODA ROOM

This room takes its name from the 18th century pagodas, fashioned from mother-of-pearl, that stand here. Many of the paintings in the room are portraits and a number are of great importance to the Cecil family history.

The portrait by Marcus Gheeraerts the Younger (1561–1636), of William Cecil (196) shows the builder of Burghley in his robes of office as Lord High Treasurer. Beneath is a portrait of his Queen, Elizabeth I, also by Gheeraerts (197). Flanking this is an outstanding portrait of Queen Elizabeth's father, Henry VIII, by Joos van Cleve (1485–1540) (194) and beneath is a small and touching portrait of A Tudor Lady (198). Over the fire hangs a large painting, copied from the original Van Dyck by John Stone (1620–1667), of Charles II as a boy with his brothers and sisters (187). The Van Dyck original is in the Royal Collection and hangs at Windsor. The original purpose of the two small closets is not known, presumably they were features of the long gallery and were incorporated when the West range was altered in 1675. One closet was transformed into a small bathroom in Victorian times and both are now laid out as they would have been in the early 20th century, incorporating clothes and accessories that belonged to the 5th Marquess and Marchioness. To the right of the door into the next room is a charming portrait of Lancelot 'Capability' Brown by Sir Nathaniel Dance (1735–1811) (211). Brown worked extensively at Burghley in the late 18th century, transforming the existing formal gardens into the parkland landscape that can be seen today. Above the door is Walker's portrait of Oliver Cromwell (192) who stormed and occupied the house in 1643.

Thomas, 1st Earl of Exeter, English School c. 1610.

Young girl thought to be Lady Georgi-Anna Cecil. Circle of Wybrand de Geest. c. 1617.

Robert Devereux, Earl of Essex, attributed to Isaac Oliver. (d.1617).

Henry VIII by Joos van Cleve.

Oliver Cromwell by Robert Walker (1605–1656). Traditionally this portrait was presented to the house by Cromwell, following his occupation of 1643.

The Blue Silk Bedroom

The splendid state bed almost fills this small room.

It was supplied to the 9th Earl by Mayhew and Ince, one of the more important London furniture manufacturers and suppliers of the 18th century. The canopy and headboard are in the 17th century style, the canopy being covered with velvet, skilfully applied to a heavily carved wood frame. The bedspread and headboard are decorated with English crewel work. The extremely fine set of furniture comprising a cabinet, two stands and a table, was purchased by the 5th Earl from the Gobelins workshop of Pierre Gôle. Gôle was one of the principal furniture makers to King Louis XIV and it is thought that this furniture may have originally been intended for the Château de Vincennes. Dating from 1665, these are some of the earliest known examples of French floral marquetry.

The cabinet by Pierre Gôle is one of the most outstanding items in the house. For years it loitered unrecognised outside the gent's loo on the ground floor. It took the visit of Professor Lunsingh Scheurleer from Leyden to identify it correctly. Suddenly imbued with previously unthought-of grandeur, it was first whisked to the conservators and then to the place of honour which it now occupies.

Below: Detail of the central 'tabernacle' cupboard of the Gôle cabinet.

THE BLUE SILK DRESSING ROOM

The 18th century Chinese export lacquer table in the centre of the room has fold-over flaps to enable it to be used for backgammon, chess, cards and as a tea table.

The chairs are part of a large set of George III painted beechwood bedroom furniture. To the left of the fireplace is a delightful small painting of ***The Virgin and Child*** by Orazio Gentileschi (1563–1639) (221). This painting was greatly admired by the 9th Earl when it was in the possession of Pope Clement XIV. He subsequently persuaded the Pope to swap the painting for a telescope! The blue and white porcelain arranged on the chimneypiece is mainly Chinese, much of it mentioned in the two inventories of 1688 and 1690 and displayed in a typically 17th century style following the designs of Daniel Marot. On the right hand chest-of-drawers are two rare Dutch earthenware bulbous pots decorated in enamels on a white ground to give the impression of Chinese porcelain. These were made in the late 17th century when European potters were incapable of equalling the wares flooding into the West from the Far East. Hanging in the window bay are Italian mosaic and pietra-dura panels purchased in Italy by the 9th Earl. From the window there is a fine view of 'Capability' Brown's lake and the Lion Bridge.

THE FIRST GEORGE ROOM

This is the first of the great State Rooms on the South side of the house. The 5th Earl employed the Italian, Antonio Verrio, to paint the magnificent ceilings.

The First George Room ceiling by Antonio Verrio.

At the time of the 5th Earl's death in 1700, this room and the tiny Jewel Closet that leads off it were the only rooms that were finished. The 9th Earl completed the decoration of the George rooms at the end of the 18th century and they were refurbished by the 2nd Marquess for the visit of Queen Victoria and Prince Albert in 1844. The furnishing and decoration of these rooms is of the finest quality, even including silver mounts to the fireplaces. The small chest-of-drawers and the bureau Mazarin are very fine examples of 17th century furniture made in the style of André Boulle featuring intricate brass fretwork inlaid into tortoiseshell. Of all the remarkable paintings here one of the finest is Christ Blessing the Bread and Wine by Carlo Dolci (1616–1686) (265) which hangs in the Jewel Closet.

Above: Christ in the house of Simon the Pharisee by Giovanni Battista Gaulli (1639–1709). Below: Our Lord Blessing the Bread and Wine by Carlo Dolci hanging in the Jewel Closet.

Left: This early painting of The Virgin and Child by Joos van Cleve (1485–1540) was purchased by the 9th Earl from the unscrupulous 18th century picture dealer James Byres as being painted by Leonardo da Vinci.

Below: The Jewel Closet ceiling by Antonio Verrio.

THE THIRD GEORGE ROOM

This room contains a number of highly important paintings and pieces of rare furniture.

The magnificent pair of still life paintings by the Neapolitan master Giuseppe Recco (1634–1695) (309 and 314) were purchased in Italy by the 5th Earl, as were the two large works by Luca Giordano (1632–1705), *The Death of Seneca* (406) and *The Rape of Europa* (397). There are also some fine pieces of furniture, particularly the set of floral marquetry commodes and corner cupboards. These were made up, using 17th century marquetry panels, by the London firm of Mayhew and Ince in 1767 at a cost of £237.15s. Mayhew and Ince worked extensively for the 9th Earl and supplied large quantities of furniture as well as working on decorative features of the house. The chairs are early 18th century in the French style and were gilded in the 19th century prior to Queen Victoria's visit.

Verrio's ceiling portrays the Reunion of Cupid and Psyche, who are surrounded by lesser deities and their attendants.

'Hearing', one of a group of Meissen figures allegorical of 'The Senses', modelled by J. J. Kaëndler c.1750.

Top right: Saint Gregory by Carlo Saraceni (1579–1620).

Middle right: one of a pair of extremely high quality marquetry commodes supplied to the 9th Earl by Mayhew and Ince in 1767.

The Death of Seneca by Luca Giordano.

THE FOURTH GEORGE ROOM

Used by Queen Victoria as a withdrawing room, this room is panelled throughout in oak.

Building records show that the dark colouring of the wood was achieved by staining with 'strong, dark ale'! The large circular table in the centre of the room is an interesting example of marquetry from different periods being combined; the square central panel is of rare 16th century Augsberg marquetry, surrounded by 18th century additions and supported by a 19th century columnar parquetry base. On the table is a late 17th century casket, decorated with tortoiseshell, ivory and silver foil. The cabinet against the rear wall, featuring pietra-dura inlay, was collected by the 5th Earl during his travels to Italy. It was a gift from his great friend, Archduke Cosimo III of Tuscany The giltwood torcheres are by Mayhew and Ince, circa 1770. Between the windows is a spectacular **Florentine pietra-dura table** (above). The inlaid top dates from the 16th century. The pair mosaic, marble and lava specimen tables that flank it were purchased in Italy in the 18th century.

The artist Verrio was an extraordinarily difficult character to manage. Fiery and unpredictable, he ground down the house Steward Culpepper Tanner, and as far as one can judge from the records, he was at odds with almost everyone in the house while he was painting the rooms. He had a keen appreciation of the naked female form and wreaked havoc among the serving girls, quarrelling along the way with the cook, whose visage was portrayed on this room's ceiling in the role of 'Plenty' - improved by the addition of four extra breasts, no doubt to her everlasting chagrin.

THE HEAVEN ROOM

Described as Antonio Verrio's greatest masterpiece, this room is decorated with scenes from ancient mythology.

A guide book written in the 19th century, describing this room refers to 'Gods and Goddesses disporting themselves as Gods and Goddesses are wont to do..!' The sheer scale of the work is astounding, the perspective so deceiving that one can almost believe in the sculptural details and extend a hand only to find the surface flat.

The figure of Verrio himself, can be seen at the far end of the room at the forge of **the one-eyed Cyclops**, sitting close to the pillar, his customary wig removed, no doubt due to the heat of his surroundings! The carpet is an English copy of a Savonnerie. The large wine cooler is a remarkable piece of Huguenot craftsmanship. Made by Phillip Rollos in 1710 it is reputedly the largest solid silver wine cooler in existence, weighing more than 230 pounds.

THE HELL STAIRCASE

The ceiling of this dark and lofty staircase was painted by Verrio as his last commission at Burghley.

Sadly, by the time he made this contract, he was heavily in debt and was unable to retain his assistants, who drifted away to more financially secure projects. Working mainly alone, this ceiling took 11 months to complete. It shows the mouth of Hell as the enormous gaping mouth of a cat and countless souls in torment within. Death, the Grim Reaper, plies his sickle amongst the unfortunates. The walls were painted by Thomas Stothard (1755–1834) over a century later. The whole impression is intended to be one of darkness and despair, in complete contrast to the preceding room.

17th century paint pots found above the painted ceilings, believed to be those of Verrio.

Years of lighting the staircase, firstly by oil and subsequently gas, had left the walls, and particularly the ceiling, with a heavy coat of soot and dirt. In 1993, a highly successful cleaning project restored this immense area to its original condition. **A small section of the legs of a female figure** at the top of the wall at the head of the stairs (right), has been purposely left to give a dramatic demonstration of the state of the ceiling before cleaning took place.

A Spanish inlaid tortoiseshell cabinet c. 1675.

The staircase, which was installed in 1786, is built from local Ketton stone. Designed using the cantilever principle and seemingly unsupported, it gives a pleasing feel of lightness in contrast to the subjects of the painted surfaces. The double stair rail was added when the house was first opened to visitors in 1957 to prevent stress to the supporting rods of the stair treads. Under the stairs is an interesting musical box made by Samuel Troll et fils in Switzerland around 1870. The ormolu mounted ebonised case is inlaid with ivory and pewter and bears the Cecil family crest.

The stairwell houses a large number of marble sculptures dating from Roman times to the 19th century. The central sculpture of A Boy carried by a Dolphin is by Joseph Nollekens circa 1766.

THE GREAT HALL

A spacious ending to the tour of the house. Over 60 feet in height with a remarkable example of a double hammer-beam roof, the hall measures 68 feet long by 30 feet wide.

Used as a banqueting hall in Elizabethan days and during the 19th century when Queen Victoria visited Burghley in 1844 as seen in this watercolour by H.B. Ziegler, it is used today for concerts and social events and provides a dignified and historic setting.

The bookcases were installed in the 19th century and contain the 17th century library collected by the 5th Earl. In the window embrasure, the large table is worthy of note; it is of Portuguese origin made from rosewood, dating from the late 17th century and is mentioned in the 1688 Inventory. The walls are hung with portraits of both members of the family and notable persons including a fine pair of 16th century portraits, in Venetian frames, of Anthony Browne, 1st Viscount Montague and his wife (354 and 356). The intricately carved clock on the rail of the Fiddlers Gallery was a gift from Lord Burghley, later 4th Marquess, to his parents. The limewood from which the surround is carved came from a lime tree in the park, supposedly planted by Elizabeth I, which fell in a great storm in 1886.

A dramatic carved detail fromthe upper part of the hammer-beam roof.

David, 6th Marquess of Exeter when Lord Burghley,
painted in Cambridge blue by Sir Oswald Birley in 1926.

LORD BURGHLEY AS SPORTSMAN

In his youth, the 6th Marquess of Exeter, known then as Lord Burghley, was a great sportsman and athlete. He went from Eton up to Magdalene College, Cambridge where he excelled in athletics and won every honour open to him.

Above: Lord Burghley's gold medal, won for the 400m hurdles, from the 1928 Amsterdam Olympics and (below), his silver medal from the 1932 Los Angeles Olympics.

A few of the trophies and medals won by Lord Burghley in his athletic career.

He won the A.A.A. 120 yards hurdles championship in 1929, 1930 and 1931 and the 440 yards hurdles title in 1926, 1927, 1928, 1930 and 1932. His time in 1927 of 54.2 seconds established a new world record though it was beaten on the same day in the U.S.A. Lord Burghley's victory in the 1928 Olympics 400 metres hurdles at Amsterdam made his name internationally famous. In 1932 and 1936 he was British Olympic Captain and after the Second World War he became President of the Amateur Athletics Association and of the International Amateur Athletics Federation, and a member of the International Olympic Committee. Lord Burghley masterminded the staging of the Olympic Games in London in 1948 when he was Chairman of the Organising and Executive Committee of the Games. A true all-rounder, Lord Exeter (he succeeded to the title in 1956) was a keen rider to hounds and for a time hunted his own private pack. He became Master of the East Sussex, the Old Berkshire and the Burghley but it is as a hurdler that he is principally remembered. Lord Exeter won hundreds of medals and trophies during his sporting career but his principal achievement was winning the Olympic Gold medal in 1928 and a Silver medal in 1932. He was portrayed by Nigel Havers in the popular film Chariots of Fire. Contrary to the film's storyline, Lord Exeter held, and still retains, the record for running around Trinity College Great Courtyard whilst the clock struck 12!

Lord Burghley's running shoes from the 1928 Amsterdam Olympics.

Lord Burghley, Winner of the Gold medal, 400 metres hurdles, 30 July 1928, Olympic Games, Amsterdam.

THE PARK AND GARDENS AT BURGHLEY

Burghley is at its most impressive when seen from the North West at a distance. From this standpoint the massive scale of the house can be best appreciated but from whatever angle one views the house, the many chimneys, the classical façades, the cupolas, balustrading and the pyramidal clock tower all group themselves into a seemingly infinite number of compositions like a kaleidoscope.

Capability Brown's summer house is modelled on an Elizabethan banqueting house at Chipping Campden, Gloucestershire.

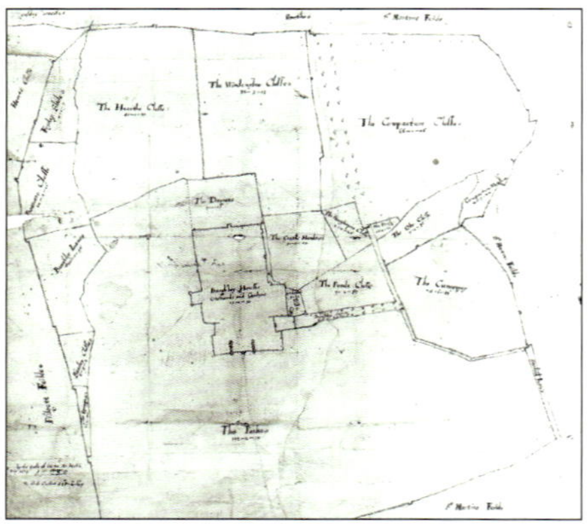

Thomas Thorpe's Survey of the Park in 1623.

Burghley is an Elizabethan house and its garden would have been very different at the time of its completion from its present appearance. In 1623 the park and gardens occupied 448 acres but in 1796 a great new intake brought the total acreage up to 1,400 acres which necessitated extending the Park wall by 3 miles. This is the wall which can be seen from the Great North Road.

The overall area of the roofs at Burghley is approximately 1½ acres, half of this being lead and the remainder local Collyweston slate. There are 76 chimneys! In Elizabethan times the main roof was used as an area for recreation; marvellous views, away from the smell from the drains and giving the opportunity for private discussions.

Fashions in gardening and landscape changed from time to time and when the 5th Earl died in 1700, work was in hand laying out the South front with 'canals, rising flights of terraces, ornamental fish-ponds, a maze, vineyard and other conceits'. The work was carried out by George London, the mentor and partner of Henry Wise, the Superintendent of the Royal gardens at Hampton Court and gardener to Queen Anne and afterwards to George I. London's final work at Burghley in 1702 was Queen Anne's Avenue - a mile-long double bank of 1,200 limes.

All this was swept away, with the exception of the lime avenues, by the 9th Earl, who following fashion, employed 'Capability' Brown (right), to landscape the park. Brown altered the contours, removing small hills and making others. He also constructed the 22-acre lake and in 1775, the Lion Bridge. The dramatic Bottle Lodges, the main entrance gates to Burghley, were designed by a Stamford architect, W. D. Legg, for the 1st Marquess of Exeter in 1801.

Lancelot 'Capability' Brown by Sir Nathaniel Dance (1735–1811) (Pagoda Room).

Capability Brown's Lion Bridge.

The Gardens of Surprise

The Gardens of Surprise feature two complementary gardens side by side. The Garden of Surprises which opened in 2007, was conceived jointly by Lady Victoria Leatham, daughter of the 6th Marquess of Exeter, and George Carter. It is an acknowledgement of William Cecil's love of gardens and was inspired by descriptions of the garden he developed at his house in Hertfordshire, Theobalds, which featured fountains with concealed pipes to spray passers by, a maze, statues, grottoes, a sundial, obelisks and formal gardens. This type of garden with "tricks and conceits" was common enough in 1560 and was created by "Modern Elizabethans", men whose fascination with astrology, astronomy and mathematics influenced all that they did, and whose knowledge of classical civilisations gave them the designs they used in their buildings and gardens.

MARTIUS
APRILIS
MAIUS
IUNIUS
IULIUS
AUGUSTUS
THE LONGITUDE DIAL
William Andrewes
Concord, Massachusetts
DAYLIGHT SAVING TIME
MIDSUMMER SUNRISE

Garden of Surprises

The Sculpture Garden

The Sculpture Garden covers 12 acres that have been reclaimed from scrub woodland and transformed into a planted area with mown paths and a lakeside walk. This secluded garden contains a core collection of contemporary sculptures and many other pieces are displayed as part of an annual exhibition.

THE WORKINGS OF THE ESTATE

The significant cost of managing and preserving Burghley House and Burghley Park is met by revenue generated by the Burghley Estate. The original estate was accumulated by Richard Cecil, father of the 1st Lord Burghley, who benefited from the dissolution of the monasteries and his marriage to the heiress Jane Heckington of Bourne. The land and associated wealth was consolidated and considerably augmented by William Cecil, 1st Lord Burghley, in the 16th century and his subsequent heirs. The Estate in its current form was endowed to Burghley House Preservation Trust by the 6th Marquess of Exeter in 1987 and is made up of some 8,500 acres of farmland, 700 acres of woodland, over 150 residential properties, 60 commercial properties (including hotels, pubs, offices and workshops), as well as quarries, sporting rights, gardens and allotments. The Estate is centred in the beautiful market town of Stamford, Lincolnshire and spreads to the outlying villages of Pilsgate, Barnack, Collyweston, Easton, Barrowden and Wakerley. Revenue is generated through letting property and other investments. The work of the Estate also includes the maintenance and restoration of Burghley House and the many interesting and historic buildings that the Trust owns. The Estate also puts great emphasis on countryside management.

In this modern age there is a delicate balance between ensuring that Burghley's countryside management meets the needs of modern agricultural production, whilst retaining its unique historical character and landscape. This is achieved by a partnership with tenant farmers on the wider Estate and a dedicated team of foresters who focus on the Park and the land immediately surrounding the House. Burghley also retains the services of specialist local contractors, skilled in hedge cutting, hedge laying, drystone walling, Collyweston slating, tree planting, tree felling, tree surgery and fencing.

CONSERVATORS AND RESTORATION

The stables at Burghley, designed and built by 'Capability' Brown in the late 18th Century, were unoccupied for many years. To make good use of these splendid buildings, they have been internally refurbished, although retaining all of their original features, and let to conservators and craftsmen as workshops. The Stable Courtyard now forms a centre of excellence of conservation and restoration that is second to none in the country. The presence of such talented workmanship at Burghley allows the Trust to make significant improvements to the preservation of its fine art collection.

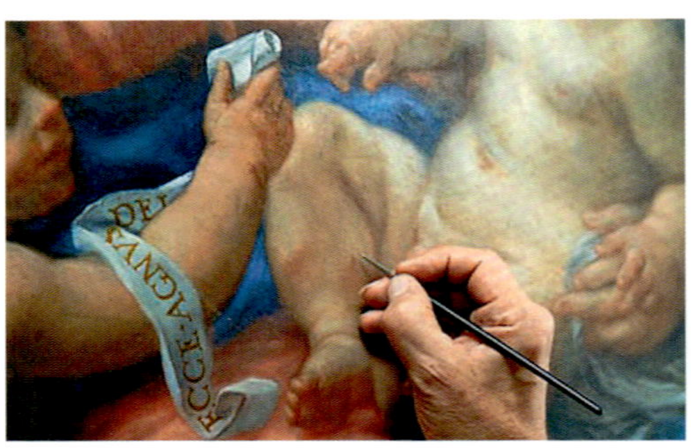